SOBRIETY

Real Talk About My Experience, Strength, and Hope

B. A. NONYMOUS

WordsmithMojo Publishing

eBook ISBN-13: 978-1-7352633-4-2
Paperback ISBN-13: 978-1-7352633-5-9

The information in this book is my interpretation of the program of
Alcoholics Anonymous based upon my experience and the experiences
of others. It should not be construed as anything approaching 'Official'
Alcoholics Anonymous dogma, nor is it an officially sanctioned piece
of "AA-approved literature".

Published by WordsmithMojo Publishing
Emmett, Idaho

INTRODUCTION

I have long wanted to write a book that would help those desiring to get sober and stay sober overcome some of the initial reservations that we all had in the beginning. I assure you that all of us had many of the same feelings of doubt, despair and demoralization that, if you are reading this book, you likely have.

But I wanted to wait until I found the perfect balance before I embarked on such an endeavor. I wanted to make certain that I had enough time in sobriety and had accumulated a wide breadth of experiences in sobriety. But I also wanted to be young enough, in sobriety, to really remember what it was like when I first came into the rooms of Alcoholics Anonymous. I wanted to really remember what my life before sobriety was like, to have a solid understanding of what happened, and of course, enough long-term sobriety to share what life can become if you choose this way of life.

If you are anything like me, you aren't at a high point in your life while reading this. None of the alcoholics or addicts that I have come across over the years came in on a winning streak. Many of us had nowhere else to go, we had tried everything else to avoid having to come into the rooms. We were all beaten down, broken and lost.

We needed to be! One doesn't make this kind of transformation if life is humming along perfectly.

Whether you bought this book, or someone bought it for you, it is likely that you need to hear some of what is contained in these pages. I know you aren't eager, but this is a short book and you just might take something away from it that will be life-changing.

This is my experience, but much of it is a shared experience with my fellows in sobriety, as we beat the odds and not only survived, but thrived in our new life of freedom and of uncluttered purpose.

I sincerely hope that you will join me on this journey.

P.S.- For the record, I don't care if you are an addict, keep reading. It all still applies to you. The further along I get in this program the more I realize that I was addicted to MORE; more booze, more cocaine, more pizza, more of whatever. The actual substance is largely irrelevant. The gift of our program is that it will help you just the same... if you choose to follow the path.

Chapter One

HOPELESS

I wanted to die, more than I wanted to live. My life had become immensely complicated and unmanageable. I had lost my business. My family had left. Most of the law enforcement members in my county knew my name. I had attempted suicide three times in an effort to end the pain, and ended up in the psych ward a couple of times. Worse was the disappointment that I could see in the eyes of everyone that was important to me.

It wasn't always that way, of course. It used to be that I was the center of the party and made sure everyone had a great time. Sure, I drank a bit too much, but that's what people did.

Over time, almost subconsciously, it stopped being about the fun, or the party. I isolated from my friends, especially those that didn't drink like I did. I drank on the way home from work and at home after work. When the excessive drinking began to take a toll on my marriage, I started to hide it. I was a professional drunk and I was still drinking a fifth of whisky most every night, while only occasionally getting caught.

As the relationship soured, so did my zest for life, my will to expend the effort to do the things that I loved; I stopped writing and playing guitar for the last four years of my drinking career. I stopped being present as a father, and my wife knew that by eight o'clock at night there was no point in talking to me, I wasn't going to remember it anyway.

As the depression deepened, my hopes for salvaging the life that I could see slipping away faded, but the bottle always helped me forget my problems. Then one day, even that stopped helping. I was a walking and stumbling ball of anger. I either ignored, or lashed out at, those I loved.

Though I had escaped entanglement with law enforcement for nearly all of my life, up until that point, I was taken into custody five times in the last six months of my drinking, three times to the county jail and twice to the psych ward at the local hospital for suicidal evaluation.

One particularly bad night, I left the house and parked at a nearby park. I swigged down the last of my tumbler full of whiskey, pulled out my Springfield .40

caliber handgun, pressed it against my temple and pulled the trigger... it clicked and misfired. I was so disheartened that I immediately vomited out the window of the car. I have put over five thousand rounds of ammunition through that gun, both before and since. It has never misfired again. But that night it misfired.

I was frikkin' immortal, apparently, which was just my luck because all I wanted to do was die and end it all.

The next morning, in a stupor, I had the thought: *maybe there is a reason I didn't die. Maybe there is something else that has a plan.* That was a profound thought for someone who had no religious background to speak of and had no thought of a God or anything else. I can't even say for sure if I believed God existed or not, but I knew that if he did, he hated me and I hated him more. But in that moment, that was the only answer that I could come up with. *Maybe there was a reason.*

Even then, at that low point, I wasn't done. I continued to linger in my alcoholic ways. A few weeks later, after an argument with my wife, I left the house angry. Angry at her, angry at myself, angry at whatever entity wouldn't let me die. I stopped and got another bottle. Three hours later I was lying unconscious in the sand and broken glass having rolled my SUV seven or eight times on the interstate, out in the middle of the desert.

My first thought when I came to was: *Oh shit, I lived.*

Some bandages, another set of handcuffs, and another night in jail. Certainly, this was my bottom, right? My wife bailed me out and we talked on the way home. I agreed to go see a drug and alcohol counselor, and maybe a few AA meetings.

I went to see the counselor a few times. She didn't understand me. She wasn't an alcoholic. She learned her stuff out of a textbook. She had no understanding of what it was really like. Admittedly, I didn't give her much of a chance.

I went to a few AA meetings, too. It was a great excuse to get out of the house. I sat in the back and tried not to make eye contact with anybody. I watched the clock until the meeting was over, then raced to my car and poured a cocktail into my tumbler for the drive home. It made for a good excuse for a little while. "I'm sorry. I'm really trying. I've gone to counselors and meetings; it just isn't working."

Clearly, I wasn't done. That may have been a low point, but it wasn't my bottom. It would take three more months and another suicide attempt, not to mention losing my family, before I was ready and willing to take action, for myself.

And doing it for myself, instead of for some judge, or ex-wife, or wife, made all the difference.

So, this is how it was for me. I share this, not to talk about myself, but to show that if you can relate to any part of my story, you should probably keep reading. Whether you think you had it better, or worse, is largely irrelevant. The whole point is that no matter where you fall on the spectrum, if it worked for a drunk like me, there is hope for you.

*"**Rarely, have we seen a person fail who has thoroughly followed our path**."*- this stanza is read at virtually every meeting of Alcoholics Anonymous, from Chapter 5 in the Big Book of *Alcoholics Anonymous*, called 'How it works'.

Let it be a reminder, that though you probably have doubts (I know I did), if you follow the suggestions that you are given and thoroughly follow our path, you have a really good chance of changing your life for the better. Because it is absolutely true. I have never seen anyone who thoroughly and continuously followed the suggestions of the program go back to their old way of life. Relapse might indeed be a part of your journey, but it doesn't have to be.

Chapter Two

FEAR

Big, macho guys like me aren't supposed to be afraid of anything. On the surface, I was all calm, cool, and collected. Underneath, the self-loathing and the disappointment in my continual and worsening failings as a 'man', as a husband, as a father, and as a business person ate away at my guts.

I didn't necessarily care (at that point) about my failed promises to my wife, family, and clients. It was the unfulfilled promises that I made to myself that hit me the hardest. No matter how many times I promised myself that it wouldn't happen again, that *this time I really mean it*... I simply couldn't 'NOT DO IT AGAIN'.

As my self-esteem plummeted, my ego worked overtime trying to keep up the appearance that everything was fine. This expressed itself as anger, tension, and a very short fuse. Everybody pissed me off, because they didn't do things right (my way), or the world was working against me. I was a good guy; I just drank a bit too much. I didn't deserve this much grief in my life. But I had all the answers, and if people would just listen to me everything would be just fine. If everyone would just leave me alone everything would be just fine.

I knew deep inside that I needed to quit drinking before it destroyed my life, but I was afraid. Afraid of admitting that I had a problem. Afraid of people finding out that I wasn't quite as 'put-together' as I appeared. Afraid of asking for help. Afraid of losing business. Afraid of going to rehab, and even more afraid that they would make me go to AA meetings.

Afraid that if it didn't work, if I couldn't get sober, that the whole thing would simply add one more failure to the list.

I was afraid of the 'G' word. Remember, I had been to a few AA meetings in the past, at the behest of others. I knew that the third step mentioned God, and I didn't want to become part of some bible-thumping religious group. That stuff just wasn't for me.

But you know what? Just like most of the things in my life I had worried about and been fearful or anxious about, it didn't happen. Once I finally gave in and surrendered, at least to the fact that there really weren't any other viable options, I went to a meeting and actually listened.

I heard men and women laughing at what outsiders would consider to be horrific stories. I laughed too, because I had had similar experiences and I could relate. Eventually, it dawned on me that everyone there must have had a similar experience which is why they could relate, and laugh, about such a personal event. I understood these people that I was so fearful of joining, and that meant that there was a chance that they understood me too. A chance...

It was three or four speakers into that first meeting before I even heard the 'G' word, but it wasn't in reference to the all-mighty, fire and brimstone creator that I had learned about as a kid. It was personal. A personal God, or higher power that the speaker believed he had a relationship with; his higher power.

It was something completely different than what I thought it would be. The entire meeting was different, though I had been in that same room in years past. This time it was different. Or was it?

Perhaps I was different. Not different from the other people in the room, no. Different from when I had last been in the room. I had been through more. I had experienced tremendous pain in those ensuing years, tremendous loss. I had done horrendous things those final months of my drinking career and crossed lines that I never thought I would cross.

Today I am grateful for those experiences, and the pain, and the loss. For without going through them... without experiencing the total demoralization and overwhelming guilt and shame about the wreckage that my life had become, I don't know if I would have ever gotten to a place where I was open enough and broken enough to try something different. To be willing to take guidance and follow suggestions... to listen.

Chapter Three

TAKE THE LEAP

Before we go any further about what the program of
Alcoholics Anonymous is (or isn't), let's take a step
backward and discuss the notion of sobriety. What
does it mean? How can you get it? And, do you even
want to?

Amongst other definitions, the simplest in this
context is:

To be Sober = to Not be drunk

Sounds simple, right? Well, it is. And it isn't.

Technically, just don't drink (or use) and you are
sober. And perhaps that is enough at this point. But to
understand living a life in sobriety we need to look a bit
deeper.

Sobriety for me, is a separate thing from simply not

drinking. However, you cannot attain it while you are still drinking.

What I mean is that true sobriety is a way of living; whereas 'not drinking' is simply not drinking.

I know several alcoholics who were miraculously able to stop drinking on their own —the white-knuckle approach—for as long as a decade without working any kind of support system or program. So, I know that it can be done.

The thing is that they may have quit drinking, but nothing else changed. They were still the same depressive, angry, petulant people that they had been before. In fact, for many this state of dry-drunkenness was even worse and more demoralizing than being drunk had been because at least drunk they had an excuse and a way to momentarily escape from the train wreck that was their life. One of them had ten years 'sober' and ended up with a gun in his mouth before finally submitting to trying something different: asking for help.

Sobriety, true sobriety, for me was a cosmic shift, not only in my actions (i.e. not drinking or using) but also in my mindset. In the way I think, the way I feel, and the way that I act. In the way that I live my life. I went from being a manic depressive, drunken buffoon, and a self-centered ball of anger to being a man at peace with himself and the world around him. A man who jumps in to help those who need it, and is unafraid of asking for help when he needs it. I went from being a giant ball of negative energy, to someone who has a steady, daily, positive outlook even when life throws us curveballs.

Life still happens and it isn't always easy, but the way that I react to things has changed.

One of my early mentors used to say, "You feel the way you feel because you think the way that you think. If you want to change the way you feel, you have to change the way that you think."

You see, if you are an alcoholic (or addict) of my type you will soon realize that alcohol is but a symptom. The real problem has always been me. It took me a while to understand that, so don't fret if you are not there yet. Either way, there is no way, that I am aware of, to treat the underlying problem while one is still drinking and/or using. My brain, and therefore my thinking, was effectively pickled from twenty-nine years of excessive drinking. I had to get the mind-altering substances out of my system and let my brain 'heal' before I could even figure out who I was, much less make drastic changes.

These are all things that I can see now, with the 20/20 vision of hindsight, I didn't recognize any of this when I was where you are now. That is why I have broken Sobriety into three distinct phases: Stop

Drinking & Get Clean, Get Honest, and Live in Sobriety.

Keep reading as I give you a quick glimpse inside the rooms, followed by a breakdown of the three phases of sobriety and I will share mistakes I made along the road to recovery, in hopes that you can learn from them.

Chapter Four

IN THE ROOMS

There are a number of ways to stop drinking. There are a number of programs which can help you get sober. These vary somewhat and so do their long-term success rates. It seems that every year there is a new fad recovery center promising to "Cure" you. I don't want to mislead you or make you think that Alcoholics Anonymous is the only way to stop drinking. It isn't.

It is, however, the only program with a nearly 80-year track record and millions of alcoholics who have succeeded in beating their demons are living a better, more productive life because of it. It is also the only program that is readily available in nearly every city and town in North America and all over the world. And it is FREE.

It worked for me and I will be forever grateful for the rooms of Alcoholics Anonymous.

First start with a Google search of, '*AA meetings in* _____ (your town)' and find a list of meetings. In larger cities there will be an overwhelming number of meetings. In small towns, not so much. But get a list of meetings, it just might save your life.

I got sober in Tucson, Arizona and we had over 400 meetings a month to choose from. In my current small town in southern Idaho we have three meetings per week, though I often attend meetings in neighboring towns which have more variety.

Once you have a list you will see there are many types of meetings: Open meetings, Closed meetings, Discussion meetings, Speaker meetings, Women's meetings, Big Book Study meetings, Step Study meetings, Meditation meetings, and many potential others. These variations provide a diverse experience, though some are better suited to choose once you have some sobriety under your belt. But ultimately, when you NEED a meeting, go find a meeting. Any meeting will do.

My advice to newcomers is to initially choose a discussion group close to home, if possible. Make life easy on yourself. That group may or may not end up being your 'regular' meeting, but it is a good place to start.

AA meeting rooms are often in low-cost places: low end strip malls, church basements, industrial parks, etc.

Don't be discouraged by the location. Remember, AA is not some corporate entity that provides meeting locations, the locations are fully funded by the people that attend the meetings, so keeping costs manageable is critical to keeping the doors open for the next alcoholic that needs to find recovery and sobriety.

One of the lessons I learned early on in my sobriety was that, no matter whether I thought it was a good meeting or a bad one, I ALWAYS feel better walking out the door than I did walking in. And truthfully, the longer I am sober the less often I judge a meeting as bad. I always get something out of a meeting, even now. But it wasn't always like that. When I was where you are right now, I was scared, embarrassed, ashamed, and hesitant. Very hesitant.

So, what can you expect?

Get to the meeting ten to fifteen minutes prior to start time, especially if you haven't been to that particular meeting before. The last thing that you need when you are already full of anxiety about going, is to walk in after they have started and have embarrassment added to your list of emotions. But by getting there early, you have time to make a cup of coffee and introduce yourself to some of the regulars before the meeting. It takes the pressure off.

As for the room itself, they vary in the way they are set up. Many have a central table (or tables) with chairs around it and more chairs along the wall. Some have chairs set up in rows. It really depends on the size of the meeting and the configuration of the meeting room.

If you want to get sober, chose a chair at the table or, if there are rows, sit in the first couple of rows. We used to call the back row "Relapse Row" because that's where people hide who are on 'court cards' and have no desire to actually participate. If you want to get sober, then join the herd not the outliers.

One thing that doesn't vary (much) is the people. You will find people from all walks of life from doctors to paupers, lawyers to homeless folks, bikers to hippies. All races, ages, and genders are susceptible to the demons of alcoholism, and all of them are represented in the rooms of AA. But the amazing thing is that you will see how they all relate to each other, they laugh, they joke, they hug. They genuinely care about one another.

If you stick around long enough to see the similarities, instead of the differences in people you will realize that in no place else on the planet are you more accepted than in an AA meeting. You will begin to see and hear the similarities in their stories too. You will see people laughing about horrific events, crazy stories, and wild experiences that would make most normal people blanch. The difference is that people aren't usually laughing at someone's story because it is funny in and of itself. Nor are they making fun of the person. They are usually laughing because they have been there and done the same stupid shit. They are laughing at themselves.

The program teaches us not to take ourselves so seriously. Our egos become small enough that we can laugh about many things that we would have been very defensive about in our drinking days.

So, expect laughter. Expect comradery from people that probably wouldn't have associated with each other in the past, but now share a common bond and common experiences which bring them together.

None of us came into the rooms on a winning streak, and most of us didn't want to be here when we got here.

So, arrive early, introduce yourself, sit with the herd, and search for similarities. That is my advice. Give it a real shot. It can change your life.

Chapter Five

PHASE ONE- STOP DRINKING & GET CLEAN

It sounds easy doesn't it?

Of course, it isn't that easy but it is doable if you are willing to follow some simple suggestions. After all, if this was something that you could do yourself you wouldn't need my advice or the program. But if you are reading this book there is a high probability that you have tried to change your ways before, yet here you are. I get it. We all do.

The paradox is that there are so many tools available within the program of Alcoholics Anonymous that make it easier to NOT drink, but in order to grasp them we need to stop drinking first.

Though every situation is different there are a few suggestions that can help you with the transition. It isn't fun, I won't lie. Detoxing from alcohol is different for everyone. The withdrawal can manifest itself as something akin to a mild hangover, or a death-defying sickness of both body and mind, or somewhere in between.

According to WebMD, "*Alcohol has what doctors call a depressive effect on your system. It slows down brain function and changes the way your nerves send messages back and forth. Over time, your central nervous system adjusts to having alcohol around all the time. Your body works hard to keep your brain in a more awake state and to keep your nerves talking to one another. When the alcohol level suddenly drops, your brain stays in this keyed-up state. That's what causes withdrawal.*"

Around 5% of alcoholics have seizures during the detox process, if you have any inkling of something resembling a seizure go to the Emergency Room and let them aid in your detox.

Shakes and nausea are quite common, few have hallucinations. I cannot overstress the importance of keeping yourself well hydrated during detox.

The most common thread amongst nearly all of the alcoholics that I have spoken to over the years is a fatigue caused by exhaustion coupled with an inability to turn off your racing mind. Your brain simply won't shut off. And, of course, in the midst of detoxing people are usually dealing with some emotional trauma, shame, and guilt surrounding the events that led them to this point anyway. A racing mind in that psychological condition is really the last thing that you need, but expect it and understand that this too shall pass... eventually.

I tell you all of this, not to scare you, but to prepare you for the possibilities. The physical and mental toll of the detox process is something that isn't discussed much and it can be a big impediment to getting sober if you don't know what to expect.

For most people, the primary withdrawal symptoms will recede in about 24-72 hours, though some may linger longer.

The silver-lining of a bad withdrawal is that once you get through it, the memory of it can be used as a deterrent to relapsing in the early days. No matter how you feel, if you decide to drink again you know that you will have to go through detox again. You really don't want to put yourself through that.

Now that I have painted a picture of how bad it can be, I want you to know that for most people it is little more than a bad hangover. Except, you have to let the hangover run its course instead of numbing it with the *hair-of-the-dog*. Drink plenty of water and something which can help restore electrolytes in your system. Also, have a couple of candy bars handy. Sugar and alcohol affect some of the same portions of your brain. In the early days of sobriety, sometimes a candy bar can help kill the cravings for alcohol. After all, much of the alcohol is converted to sugar aldehydes once it is metabolized.

Don't be surprised, regardless of your normal dietary habits if you begin craving sugary treats. I would also suggest you give into that temptation during the first few weeks, because while too much sugar is certainly not good for you, alcohol is trying to kill you. Opt for the better choice.

Even though I mentioned it previously, let me reiterate... If you are an addict the symptoms might vary slightly, but the message is the same. In fact, alcohol withdrawal is potentially more dangerous than drug withdrawal. But the point is, you need to get clean and sober in order to gain the gifts of the program.

Clear-headedness takes a bit, and working the program takes clear-thinking. Making good choices in your life takes clear thinking too.

Even if you are struggling to stop drinking, start going to meetings. Try not to be drunk at the meeting, but go, sit, and listen. The third tradition of Alcoholics Anonymous states that the "only requirement for membership is a DESIRE to stop drinking." A desire. Decide that you want to stop. ONLY YOU can decide this. Not your husband, not your wife, and not some judge. The landscape is littered with alcoholics that think that AA didn't work for them. The real truth is that it didn't work, because they didn't work AA.

Remember the quote in Chapter One? *Rarely, have we seen a person fail who has THOROUGHLY followed our path*.

What is *"our path"*? More importantly how do you follow it?

When you first begin going to meetings (and listening) you will hear people talking about the 12 Steps. The program of Alcoholics Anonymous is written out in the first 164 of the Big Book, but it has been summarized into twelve action steps which are often printed on a poster and hanging on a wall in AA meeting rooms.

In fact, depending on which month you decide to get sober the topic in many rooms will vary. Since there are twelve months in the year and there are twelve steps in the Big Book of Alcoholics Anonymous the meeting topics will often be Step One related in January, Step Two related in February and so on. Don't worry about the topic. If you decide to get sober in July, your very first meeting might be about Step Seven. Don't sweat it that you don't understand it. The message will still come through loud and clear when people share. Again, listen for stories that you can relate to and experiences that sound familiar. Also listen for someone that sounds like he or she might have what you want: solid sobriety.

Now that we have clarified the point about topics you might hear, let's get back to the path.

Despite all the talk of steps and traditions, the initial path to sobriety is quite simple. It isn't easy, but it is simple.

Here are the basic actions that YOU need to take to get on the path:

- **Get a list of meetings near you**
- **Go to a meeting**
- **Get a Big Book**
- **Go to a few more meetings**
- **Try not to drink between meetings**
- **Find a Sponsor to take you through the steps**

Sounds simple enough, right?

Well, it is and it isn't. One other thing that most of us have in common is that we have a tendency to complicate things, make life more difficult than it needs to be. Most of us discover that we are our own biggest problem. If you can get out of your own way, this is simple. Let's discuss the actions further.

We already discussed getting a list of meetings. Having a list allows you some flexibility to go try different meetings and see which one feels right to you. So, either way, you need to use your list and actually go to a meeting.

One of the common fears that newcomers have when they first start going to meetings is: *What if I run into someone I know?*

Many have had that same fear. I know that I sat in the parking lot my first few meetings watching who walked in. So, I get it.

But think about this: YOU never cared who saw you stumble drunkenly into the corner store for another bottle or another 30-pack. Why would you care who saw you trying to do better? Not to mention the fact that if you run into someone you know at a meeting; it is likely because they are there for the same reasons. This is one of those things that we tend to make a bigger deal than it is. Don't sweat it.

Go to a meeting, sit at the table, or in the middle of the pack, and introduce yourself. At many, if not most meetings the person running the meeting will ask (near the beginning) if there is anyone with "less than 30-days of sobriety to introduce themselves by their first name only so the group can get to know you better." Raise your hand and introduce yourself. This isn't to put you on the spot, but to let people know that you are new to the program and might need some help and guidance. It also demonstrates that you are open to trying something different. Remember, if you could do this yourself you wouldn't be here. Follow the path.

The next action step is to get a copy of the book, *Alcoholics Anonymous*. You can order it from Amazon, or go to a used bookstore –a great source of brand new unopened Big Books thanks to those that went back out without ever opening the book. Many meetings will have them for sale at cost, too. If you truly cannot afford one, then mention that at a meeting, someone will likely help you out. Reading it is a great way to pass the time between meetings.

The first 164 pages of the Big Book are the program of AA. The bulk of the rest is made up of stories of folks who have come through the program. The book itself, written by Bill W., was first published in 1939, though it has been updated a handful of times since. (Most of you will end up with the 4th edition). You might notice a few outdated words or phrases as you read it, but even through the revisions it has retained the bulk of its original wording and messaging. Even so, it is every bit as relevant and revered today as it was back then. I highly recommend that you read ALL of it from the 'Foreword', Dr. Silkworth's letter, Bill's story, and on through at least page 164. Read on through the rest of the stories at your convenience.

Another note to addicts: I suggest you don't dwell on the fact that he mentions alcohol and drinking exclusively. Substitute your drug of choice every time he mentions booze in your head if you need to, but read on and hear the underlying message. You will find that we all share a common malady; the substance of choice is largely irrelevant.

That brings us back to 'Go to More Meetings'. It is commonly recommended that newcomers commit to going to *ninety meetings in ninety days*. Though there is ample evidence that newcomers that DO go to 90 meetings in 90 days have a significantly higher success rate in stopping drinking, I felt like it was too big of number to wrap my head around in the early days.

After all, I was trying to figure out hour-by-hour how to not drink (sometimes minute-by-minute). How could I be expected to grasp a 90-day goal?

I couldn't, that was simply too much. I tell newcomers to go to *at least* seven meetings in seven days. *At least*. But I also give them the caveat that if they are really struggling-- really having a craving or generally going crazy-- to get to a meeting ASAP, more than one per day if necessary.

If you are in a large or mid-sized city there are likely meetings throughout the day every day. Early morning meetings tend to have a high percentage of people with long-term sobriety. Noon meetings tend to heavily favor newcomers, after all those still into their addictions/or at least living in it tend to NOT get up early.

Evening meetings tend to be a good mix of both newcomers and those with strong sobriety.

I recommend that you try them all. Every meeting is a bit different. Even the same meeting can vary significantly from day to day; there may be six people at a Monday night meeting, but if you go to the same meeting on a different night, say Thursday, there might be forty or more. So, don't judge a meeting based on a single visit. Try different locations, different meeting times, and different days. They will all be a little different, we are alcoholics after all, we don't conform to any norm by nature.

As a matter of fact, this is part of the reason for the recommendation of 90 meetings in 90 days. In order to hit that many it will cause you to go to different meetings. The hope is that by the end of the 90 days you will have found a meeting that feels like home to you. We call this, not coincidentally, a Homegroup.

For me, personally, I chose to primarily go to the early morning meetings at the beginning. I lived thirty-five minutes from the meeting place and the meeting started at 6:45am every day. At the beginning it was a challenge to get up and get there, but I soon found that by starting my day at a meeting and getting in the sobriety mindset, I could carry that mindset into my day, as opposed to dragging my day into a meeting in the evening. Do what feels right to you.

But remember, you are here to change your ways. So, don't be afraid to test your comfort zone a bit. That is the only way that change occurs.

If you aren't a morning person, challenge yourself to get up and go to a few early morning meetings anyway. You'll be amazed at how much energy you have when you aren't hungover. If you are an early morning person, challenge yourself to go to evening meeting. Whatever you do, don't fall back on your old habits, challenge them. Break out of your rut, and I am talking about more than just drinking (though at this point that is the most important).

If you notice above, I discussed "if you live in a large or mid-sized city" that you have a plethora of options for meetings. In small towns it varies greatly and adds a few challenges. The size of the town rarely dictates the availability of meetings, meetings are available nearly everywhere in the U.S. and throughout much of the world, but it does dictate the number of them. For example, I got sober in Tucson (a good-sized city) and there were around 400 meeting per month to choose from (15-20 per day on average), then I moved to a small town of about 26,000 people and we had a strong AA community with 3-5 meetings/day to choose from. Now I live in an even smaller town, under 6,000 people and there are only 3 meetings per week. My small town is within 20-30 minutes of a number of other towns and cities though so I still have plenty to choose from. My current Homegroup is about 30 minutes from home, not convenient necessarily but close enough to make 3 or 4 meetings per week there.

One of the questions we are asked near the beginning of our sobriety is if we are *"willing to go to any length to get it?"* This is part of that willingness, finding a way to adapt and find positive reasons to go to a meeting rather than excuses not to.

In the first days of sobriety it is not uncommon for people to go to three or more meetings per day as they try to immerse themselves in the meetings and avoid the cravings to drink or use. It is simply a diversion, but it also works.

Many of us come in after having lost jobs and/or families. Unfortunately, for us, this leads to an awful lot of idle time on our hands which is a very dangerous position for the newly sober to be. We are still filled with shame, regret, resentments and guilt. Idle time lets us spend entirely too much time in our own heads lamenting our situation. This is really a bad idea at this point in recovery. Keep yourself busy. Meetings are a great way to do that. Go to as many meetings as you can, and try not to drink between meetings. Also get phone lists at the meetings you attend. Talking to another alcoholic can save your life. Often times the secretary/chairperson will ask if anyone needs a phone list, if they don't then ask for one when you introduce yourself as a newcomer.

That brings us to the last action step in PHASE One: Find a sponsor to guide you through the steps.

I know... you just rolled your eyes. I did too. I am an intelligent guy, surely, I could read the book and go through the steps myself, right?

Wrong! My best thoughts and plans got me drunk.

If I could have done it myself, I would have. Believe me I tried. I waited nearly four months into sobriety before I had the courage and the desperation necessary for me to ask for help. The first few months of sobriety were simply due to willpower and meetings. Sure, I learned things in the meetings, but meetings aren't 'The Program' of AA. The steps are. I knew I was half-assing it by not doing it sooner, but my ego got in my way (again). Yet, every morning at my meeting the words, from the reading of 'How it works', "*half measures availed us nothing*", jumped out and taunted me.

Finally, I decided to *surrender* to the program.

What is a sponsor?

Your sponsor will become your mentor in the program. They will be your sounding board for ideas, your spiritual guide, if you will. They will take you through the steps and the Big Book. They will talk you down when you reach your breaking point. They will advise you in life decisions and program choices.

Hopefully, they will be honest with you and call you on your bullshit. If you have reached this point, if you are anything like me, you have spent the last months and years lying to the people that care about you and more importantly lying to yourself, and not just about your drinking and using.

The alcoholic mindset creates so many deceptions that life becomes overwhelming and unmanageable. Your 'Life' story is something that you created one tiny (or big) lie or embellishment at a time. Many of us created such elaborate facades to cover our failings that we began to believe them ourselves.

In fact, when I first came into the rooms of AA, I had no idea that I didn't know who I was. I had trouble separating the fact from fiction in my story. Not surprisingly, I later discovered that I had spent 29 years minimizing my shortcomings and embellishing the good stuff to the point that I didn't even know what was true and what wasn't. If you choose a good sponsor, they will see through much of the BS—mostly because they have been there.

So, how do you find a good sponsor? You go to meetings, lots of meetings. You listen when people speak. It won't take long before you identify one or two people who really speak to you. The ones that make you sit up straighter in anticipation when they are called on to share. You might even find yourself regularly nodding along to what they are saying.

There are only a couple of rules regarding choosing a sponsor, and like most rules in AA they aren't really rules, but suggestions: Choose someone the same gender, choose someone with more than a year of sobriety, and who has gone through the steps with a sponsor themselves. I have seen exceptions work to all of those 'rules' but they are exceptions. Follow the suggestions and you will have a better shot at success.

One thing that a Sponsor will not, and cannot do, is keep you sober. A Sponsor will give you the tools of the program and the best advice they are able to give, but ultimately only you can make the decision to drink or use again. They cannot do that for you.

Ironically, it is you that are keeping them sober.

A big part of the program is to be of service and carry the message to other alcoholics. By asking them to sponsor you, you are allowing them to be of service which aides them in their sobriety... whether you stay sober or not. It truly is a symbiotic relationship; one drunk helping another drunk so the other doesn't get drunk.

Chapter Six

PHASE TWO—GET HONEST

If you have completed Phase One--Gone to meetings, bought a Big Book, gone to more meetings and found a Sponsor—then it is also likely that you have strung together a few days without drinking, maybe a week, perhaps a month. If so, congratulations! You have taken the first big stride toward living a better life (even if it doesn't feel like it yet). If not, then reach out to your Sponsor and ask for ideas.

And that's the thing, it may not feel better yet. In fact, it might feel worse. The nature of alcoholism requires more work to be done aside from simply not drinking. This is a major reason that people relapse so frequently in the early days, our lives have not changed yet, but now we can't numb and drown our sorrows in alcohol. Instead, we have to feel our feelings, some-thing we have long tried not to do. After all, booze gave us a way out of feeling most feelings. Now we have to face them, but you are not alone.

The Big Book tells us that "alcohol is but a symptom". Most of us discover over the course of just a few months that we are our own biggest problem. It's true. What's worse is that while we may be our biggest problem, we often don't have any idea who we really are, and therefore we have no realistic way to solve our biggest problem. Take away the alcohol, and we are still left with ourselves.

Once we learn how to identify and fix some of our faulty thought processes, life begins to improve on a daily basis. Like learning anything else, learning to identify and change our shortcomings takes a little time and effort. It also takes Honesty, Openness, and Willingness—the HOW of the program.

One challenge that many face in early sobriety is that we carry our baggage with us. Things from our past often make trust a difficult thing. If you cannot trust your Sponsor or people in your homegroup, well, honesty, openness, and willingness fly out the window. More than eighty years of experience has shown that those three components are critical to reaching the promises of the program and attaining true sobriety.

At the end of the day, we simply have to cease fighting everything. Doing things 'Our' way clearly didn't work. We have to surrender ourselves to the program.

Surrender doesn't come easy for us; we don't follow directions particularly well. But it is necessary. We must cease fighting against what might be our last hope for salvation, for sanity, for a life worth living. We must let go of our old ideas and truly try something new.

So how do we do that?

Start by working the steps with your Sponsor. It is difficult to cease fighting everything while we continue to hold doubt.

The first step of AA is:

We admitted we were powerless over alcohol and that our lives had become unmanageable.

This step is the only one that we must do 100% perfectly to stay sober, and it looks simple, but it does present some challenges in early sobriety and again later in sobriety unless we are vigilant. Your Sponsor will have his/her own take on this step and its importance, but let's break it down.

The first step is really made up of two parts. The first is: *We admitted we were powerless over alcohol.* It is rarely surprising to us that we are alcoholic. We have known it for years more than likely, at least deep down, despite our superpower of denial. I knew. You probably know too. Hell, some of us were proud of our alcoholic prowess until consequences began to pile up.

The interesting thing about the alcoholic mind is that despite a willingness to admit to ourselves that we are alcoholic, we tend to reflexively revolt against the word, 'Powerless'. The first step is all about willingness and coming to a belief--down in your core—that you have no ability to control your drinking for any significant period of time. We are powerless, because most of us tried every other option that we could find to keep us out of these rooms, yet here we are.

The second part can be read as: We admitted *That our lives had become unmanageable.* There are a wide swath of alcoholics in these rooms, from all walks of life. We come into these rooms from numerous points along the alcoholic spectrum, each with similar stories and thoughts but often different endpoints. I say this so that you stay focused on yourself; it is downright dangerous to compare yourself with others. After all, you only know what they want you to know. For a homeless man, hearing that someone ended up living in a crappy motel room sounds like a pretty manageable life. They might never know that that person once lived in their dream home, but lost it somewhere along the way.

I have come to view manageability as something akin to a sliding scale. Up until the last few months of my drinking career I believed that life was fairly manageable, the last few—Thankfully—made it clear to me that my life was unmanageable. After all, I wanted to die more days than I wanted to live. But here's the thing, looking back now I can see that my life had become unmanageable several *YEARS* before I got here, but I didn't notice until I was blessed with sobriety and the clear vision that comes with hindsight.

When you are in the throes of your addictions, it is amazing how far we can slide down the sliding scale before we notice. We learn to ignore, cope, numb, and blame our way to our bottom, wherever that may be.

The first step's two sides serve two purposes for us. While both are an indication of willingness, the first part *"admitted we were powerless over alcohol"* serves to both define our malady and allow us to surrender. The second part, the *unmanageability*, is our empirical evidence as we convince ourselves deep in our inner-core that the first part is true.

I mentioned earlier that this step created challenges not only for the newcomer, but in later sobriety unless we are vigilant. Unless we have thoroughly and completely done the first step and taken it into our heart, there is a chance (I have seen it more than a few times) that once life improves and we get a ways down the road to sobriety that we will forget what it was really like when we came in. We can forget how bad it was and the chaos that drove us into these rooms. If we forget the degree and depth of our terrible and incomprehensible demoralization; our cunning, baffling, and powerful nemesis can find a crack in the armor we have built up against it. Some begin to still admit that they are alcoholics but, somehow, even subconsciously decide that they might have some power over alcohol now that they have come this far. It always ends badly. Sometimes it ends fatally.

So, work with your Sponsor and do a thorough first step. It just might save your life. It will definitely improve it.

Ultimately, the first few steps are about your willingness to get honest with yourself and realize that you have a problem that you cannot solve by yourself, a grave affliction that creates chaos in your life and the lives of those around you.

Many of you have tried to limit your drinking and control it, and you may have even found a bit of momentary control, but over the course of time it falters leaving you in ever greater despair. Then many of you tried drug & alcohol counseling, outpatient rehab programs and finally inpatient treatment centers with the hopes that you could gain control, but inevitably it only worked (long-term) if you paired it with something else, the place that you have tried to avoid coming to for so long.

My experience was that I went to a counselor, then I tried an outpatient program, and my continual failure to stop drinking led me to an inpatient rehab. I, for one, was grateful for the respite that going away for a few weeks gave me, but did rehab GET me sober?

Yes... indirectly.

You see, while I may have gotten something out of rehab, the biggest thing that rehab did for me was to badger me until I went to a few AA meetings. I resisted for about ten days before relenting and agreeing to go, mostly to get my counselor off my back. There happened to be a great meeting only a mile or so from the treatment center that met at various times throughout the day. On about the third morning meeting, I stopped being spiteful about being there and stopped taking everyone else's inventory. I began to listen. I heard a couple of things that resonated so I went back the next day... and the next, and the next. When I got out of rehab, the first thing I did when I got back to my hometown, was find a list of meetings. In all the years since then, I have never again found it necessary to drink... yet.

You see, the one thing that counseling, and outpatient groups lack is sobriety. What I mean is that most counselors weren't drunks or addicts, some were but most just studied it in school. Outpatient programs too have counselors and other newcomers—not sobriety.

The difference with a meeting of Alcoholics Anonymous is you have a room full of people who have walked down the dark tunnel you have been in, but many of them have come out the other side. They have been there and can walk you through, if you choose to surrender. This isn't something that works all alone, but with the help and understanding of other alcoholics; things can be different. The first word of the first step says it all; this is a '*We*' program, not a 'me' program.

You never have to drink again, if you don't want to.

But in order to do that you must cease fighting the program. Go along with it, what have you got to lose? What other options are left for you? Why not give it a chance?

It works, it really does... if we work it.

All of this leads us to the second step:

Came to believe that a power greater than ourselves could restore us to sanity.

Again, this is about willingness. The definition of a '*power greater than ourselves*' has been intentionally left vague. Again, your Sponsor will have his/her own take on this but here's mine. A *power greater than ourselves* can be nearly anything. If you come from a religious background it can mean God, but the intent of this step is to shrink your ego a bit (maybe more than a bit) and come to believe that you don't have all the answers. For many who come into the program the power they believe in (initially) is the power of the group, or the power of the program. Remember the old adage: two heads are better than one? Same idea, a group of drunks trying to do the next right thing have more power than I do alone. In fact, many will use 'Group of Drunks' (G. O. D.) as their higher power, and call it God. Still others who fight the religious beliefs of God will use the program of Alcoholics Anonymous as their higher power by believing in the 'Good Orderly Direction' (G.O.D.) that the program and the steps provide us. Whatever you need to use as a higher power will work for now, as long as it isn't YOU.

Your best thinking got you to this point. Maybe it's time to believe that something else might have a better solution. I know of a few people that used a doorknob as their higher power. The reasoning behind it was that every time they used the doorknob to enter a meeting of AA, they got a little better. They felt a little better. Over time that meant they began to live a more 'sane' lifestyle.

One other point about Step two, notice that it doesn't say the power greater than ourselves 'Will' or 'Would' restore us to sanity. It says 'could'. It has a power that you do not possess, but it won't do anything unless you do your part: go to meetings, read the Big Book, work with your Sponsor, be of service, etc.

One of the great things about the program is the Freedom to choose. Despite the rhetoric online, and the naysayers, this "cult" doesn't tell you what to believe at all. It simply lays down a plan of actions that millions who came before you have had success with. This Freedom also allows your beliefs to evolve as you go through the program, as you grow spiritually, as you gain clarity, as you learn more about both the program and yourself.

Let's take a moment, before we get to the third step, to discuss what the program is (and what it isn't). This is NOT a religious program; it is a lifelong spiritual endeavor.

What does that mean?

Despite the fact that many meetings are held in church basements or rooms, and the fact that God is mentioned quite frequently, this is not a religious program. Some do utilize the beliefs they had prior to coming into the program. But many who grew up with religion end up un-learning what they thought they knew and coming to an entirely new understanding of their relationship with their God. Many more come in with no belief in a God or specific religion find an understanding of their own God, or higher power.

Many revolt at the word God and name their higher power, HP.

Whatever works, as long as you believe in something greater than yourself.

The best description, that I have heard, of the difference between religion and spirituality is this:

Religion is for people who are afraid of going to Hell. Spirituality is for people who have already been there.

Most of us have been there. We've lived lives of chaos, handcuffs, divorce, job instability, psych wards, depression, and more.

I, personally, wasn't really sure if I even wanted to quit drinking when I first came to AA. I just wanted to stop the chaos and wreckage that I had created. I wanted peace of mind, which I would later learn was serenity. I didn't want to DO anything, certainly not that 'God' thing. I simply wanted to quiet my mind.

Eventually, I became desperate enough to surrender and cease fighting the program... even the God thing. Finally, I had the willingness to work the program and my life is immeasurably better because of it.

There is an entire chapter of the Big Book devoted to this discussion. Chapter 4 is called *We Agnostics* and does a great job of addressing this subject. If the 'G' word is getting in the way of your recovery, perhaps it would be a good idea to read that first.

Which brings us to Step Three:

Turned our will and our lives over to the care of God, as we understood him.

I used the words in this step as a reason NOT to come into the rooms for years. Honestly, that is the only regret that I still hold onto from my past. Had I had someone explain this in terms that I could understand, then I would be that much further along on my journey. But I have also come to understand that I wasn't meant to yet, I needed to go through my complete mental, emotional, spiritual, and physical collapse before I was able to try something different. I needed to be broken and beaten down and completely desperate before I was willing to do that. I can be stubborn that way.

Turning *our will and our lives over to the care* of something that we don't believe in is a difficult thing. Heck, even if we did believe, giving up our will is a challenge, period.

But let's go back to the example of the doorknob. Aren't you turning your will and your hopes for a better life over to the doorknob every time you go to an AA meeting? You are doing something you don't really want to do (at the beginning, at least) in hopes that it will help you stop drinking and improve your life. You don't KNOW that it will work, but you have come to believe that it could. So, day after day you turn the doorknob and walk into a meeting.

The same faith can be used if you use the *Group of Drunks* as your G. O. D.; aren't you giving up your will and putting your faith in the group every time you go to the meeting as you seek guidance to help you get or stay sober? Don't you have a small hope that you can attain what some of those people have? After all, it worked for them, maybe it can work for you too.

It is no different with *Good Orderly Direction* as your G.O.D., putting the faith in the actions you learn from the program. Again, if it worked for that room full of drunks it might just work for you.

The real point is, don't let one word keep you from reaching your potential. Ironically, you are giving it the power to do that by resisting. Get rid of your old ideas regarding God, if you need to, and make it something that you can understand and work with. Remember, your understanding of your higher power can and will evolve. You aren't making a sacred pact with some deity; you are simply admitting that you don't have all the answers, but you have the willingness to find them.

The first three steps are all about willingness: admitting you don't have control, believing that something greater than yourself might, and tuning your self-will out as you turn your future life over to that something.

Our egos, despite the low self-image and self-inflicted misery, are often surprisingly robust. These steps are geared toward shrinking your ego, so that you are able to cease fighting the program... and everything else.

CHAPTER SEVEN -COMMON CHALLENGES

I am not going to go through all of the steps like I did the first three, that isn't the purpose of this book. That is between you and your Sponsor. This book is intended to serve as a guide to what you can expect as you come into sobriety and the program, not an all-encompassing dissertation of the program. But here is the list of the 12 Steps of Alcoholics Anonymous:

1. *We admitted we were powerless over alcohol and that our lives had become unmanageable.*
2. *Came to believe that a power greater than ourselves could restore us to sanity.*
3. *Made a decision to turn our will and our lives over to the care of God as we understood him.*
4. *Made a searching and fearless moral inventory of ourselves.*

5. *Admitted to God, to ourselves, and to another human being the exact nature of our wrongs.*

6. *Were entirely ready to have God remove all these defects of character.*

7. *Humbly asked him to remove our shortcomings.*

8. *Made a list of all persons we had harmed, and became willing to make amends to them all.*

9. *Made direct amends to such people wherever possible, except when to do so would injure them or others.*

10. *Continued to take personal inventory and when we were wrong promptly admitted it.*

11. *Sought through prayer and meditation to improve our conscious contact with God as we understood him, praying only for knowledge of his will for us and the power to carry that out.*

12. *Having had a spiritual awakening as a result of these steps, we tried to carry this message to alcoholics and practice these principles in all our affairs.*

I do want to take a few moments to briefly discuss some potential pitfalls that we often come up against in early sobriety.

The first pitfall, a very common failure, is rushing Step Nine.

Most of us come to these rooms with a trail of wreckage behind us: broken marriages, angry spouses, pissed boyfriends, devastated kids, sad parents, distrusting employers, and disgruntled coworkers, legal issues, etc. As a matter of fact, it is often a personal relationship failure that finally drove us into these rooms.

But here's the problem, since we came in in the midst of such chaos, cleaning up that chaos (and gaining sympathy) is often the first thing that we want to do. Newcomers often get a week or two clean and sober, then want to go out and start apologizing to the people they had hurt or disappointed. They rush around apologizing to people and telling them they haven't drank in a week, so things will be better from here on out.

Step Nine states:

Made direct amends to such people wherever possible, except when to do so would injure them or others.

There is a reason that it is Step Nine, and not placed earlier in the program. Not the least of which is the fact that we have worn out the phrase "I'm sorry" amongst nearly anyone that knows us. It holds no meaning; we've likely used it hundreds and hundreds of times but never changed our ways.

Another reason is that nobody believes that you will get sober, for any length of time. They see it as a 'time-out' for your drinking career. And we have given them every reason to believe this way. How many times have you told yourself, "Never again"?

This is a program of spiritual growth; you cannot rush the process. There are no shortcuts. You get to stay sober one-day-at-a-time and hopefully you will string together some of those 24-hour periods. Work with your Sponsor and go through the program thoroughly, and when it comes time for Step Nine talk with them about each amends that you intend to make BEFORE you make it. If you rush it, the reaction you get from those people will potentially be bad enough that you give up and go back out and drink. Have patience and do your part. They aren't going anywhere; they may still be pissed when it is time for you to make amends. But you will have grown spiritually, you will have some sobriety time behind you, and you will have some guidance on how to make amends.

One other word about that. Making *amends* is not saying, "I'm sorry." The word, amends, necessitates **making a change in your behavior**.

Look at it this way: the 13th *Amendment* didn't say that we, as a country, were sorry for that whole slavery thing. It CHANGED the law and abolished slavery.

It takes time to make a meaningful change, please don't rush it. Follow the Steps, do the work that is suggested, and do your amends at the appropriate time.

A word of caution about the Fourth Step:

Made a searching and fearless moral inventory of ourselves.

There is plenty of empirical evidence that suggests if newcomers are going to go back out, it will be before or during the Fourth Step. While the first three steps are largely philosophical, Step Four requires some actual work and it makes us delve deep into the dark recesses of our heads. That can be a dangerous place to be, unless you have some help and guidance. Some people are simply lazy and didn't want to do the work, others faltered due to the emotional turmoil that can be brought out as we looked into our past. Either way, the Fourth Step seems to be the tipping point.

The good news is that if you persevere and become comfortable in the discomfort of rigorous honesty, and do a thorough Fourth and Fifth Step, your odds of staying sober go up exponentially.

Chapter Eight

PHASE THREE—LIVE IN SOBRIETY

If we are painstaking about doing the Steps, following the suggestions, and trying to do the next right thing—well, now we get to live a life in sobriety. **Getting sober has been, by far, the best decision I have ever made**.

My life today is so far ahead of my wildest dreams; however, 'life' still happens. It isn't perfect, in fact, there are times that life can be incredibly difficult. Horrible things happen, yet many of us are able to stroll through with a serenity that surprises even us. I, personally, have been through much tougher events in sobriety than I ever went through during my drinking years.

We don't drink, no matter what, period.

But it does take some time and effort to get to that point.

At some point in sobriety a switch flips; from 'I *need* to go to meetings', to 'I *get* to go to meetings'. Indeed, our entire outlook upon life changes. We learn to live in gratitude, instead of resentment.

There was a particular moment when I learned that I was grateful for the bad things that had happened too. All of my life experiences, good and bad, brought me to the place I am today. How could I regret what got me to come into the rooms of Alcoholics Anonymous? I am grateful today, for all of it.

For many, after a few years of sobriety, our program becomes about much more than just NOT drinking, though we are aware that we are only one drink away from losing it all. The program becomes one of personal growth and development with an emphasis on the growth and maintenance of our spiritual condition.

One tool that has consistently been beneficial for my state of mind... meditation.

Now mind you, I am not some hippy, new age guru. Meditation was always something I had looked at as strange. However, just days into my sobriety, whilst I was still in rehab, I found myself completely unable to relax or sleep. My mind was constantly racing and spinning in spirals of woe and regret. It was suggested by the chaplain at the rehab center that I try coming to the early morning guided meditation session. I was skeptical and I was quite convinced that he was going to try to get me to pray. I wanted no part of that.

Three days later, still unable to sleep and anxious, I finally relented. I went to the meditation. I decided *what the hell do I have to lose? I am up anyway.* This was often the way things went in my alcoholic mind. I resist until I have no other options. Let me assure you that there is, indeed, an easier way to live life. I tended to do everything the hard way.

Anyway, I went to the meditation room which had some Native American wooden flute music piped in from some unseen source, and took a seat and tried to get comfortable for what I was absolutely convinced would be a wasted forty-five minutes of my life. It was an ironic thought for someone who would later realize that he had wasted the better part of forty-five years of his life.

I sat. I looked around at the handful of other people in the room. They seemed less baffled than I, but perhaps they were more willing than I was to give it a shot. They had their eyes closed.

What the hell I thought as I closed mine and sat silently. The strange but beautiful music allowed me to get out of my own head and, at least, be present in the room for a few minutes.

Soon, a soft-spoken voice intruded on the music and prompted me to breathe slowly and deeply. Soon it directed me to count the breaths while ignoring whatever other thoughts tried to enter my consciousness. Counting from one to ten then back to one, over and over, I soon felt the tension in my body melt away long before I realized that it had left my brain too. It was an experience that I will never forget.

That night as I lay on the uncomfortable strange bed in my room at rehab, I stared at the ceiling pleading for the runaway train in my head to slow down and trying to will myself to sleep. Then I remembered the morning meditation. I closed my eyes and focused on my breathing, soon I began counting breaths. Next thing I knew it was morning and I had slept for nearly seven hours which was far longer than normal for me.

Like most worthwhile things in life, meditation took some time and practice. But over time I became able to quiet my mind at anytime, anywhere. The ability to find comfort within your discomfort, to have grace amidst the chaos in life, was an entirely new experience for me. I suspect it is hard to imagine having peace of mind in the midst of tragedy and trauma, but it is possible and it has a name... SERENITY.

Serenity was what I had been searching for my entire life, but never even noticed. Once you reach this place, the point where you truly understand what serenity is, you will yearn to hold on to it. You will do whatever it takes to keep it.

Earlier I mentioned that at some point the program ceased to be about NOT drinking. For me, this is the point that this happened. I was far more eager to keep my serenity than I was to have another drink.

The question, of course, is how do you keep this serenity?

The truth is that I don't know which of the suggestions worked for me and are still working today. Is it going to meetings, reading the big book, working the steps, talking to my sponsor, or being of service to others?

I don't know which one is the answer, so I continue to do all of them. That is what got me here, why would I change?

Acceptance is the key. Accepting the reality of any situation. Accepting responsibility for my actions. Accepting that I don't have all the answers. Accepting people as they are.

That last one is a tough one. It took me several years to understand that I had to accept people as they are for my own piece of mind. I spent most of my life judging people and/or placing expectations on them. I expected them to do things my way. I expected them to react to any given situation the way I wanted them to. For example, on the highway when I sped up the 'fast' lane, I expected the slower cars in front of me to move aside so I could pass. When they didn't, I got angry. Embarrassingly angry.

Would it have been the polite thing for them to do? Certainly.

But what they did or didn't do wasn't my real problem. How I reacted to it was my real problem. Screaming and cussing at them was harmful to me, not to them. Hell, most of the time they were oblivious to the entire episode. It was my anger that fed the darkness in my soul.

But why?

Because, apparently, the world doesn't revolve around me. Because I expected them to be courteous and they weren't. I took everything as a personal afront. Self-righteously, I demanded that they move over by flashing my lights, honking my horn, and flipping them off.

In my alcoholic brain, I didn't see this as an overreaction. I had the ability to make mountains out of mouse turds. I didn't 'go with the flow'. I expected them to do what I wanted them to do.

And it wasn't just road rage. I set, and was disappointed by, expectations for everyone in every facet of my life: Wife, parents, at work, at the grocery store, on social media, everywhere.

Expectations are the enemy of serenity. When you

place expectations on anyone, you are bound to be disappointed on a regular basis. Whether you are in the right or the wrong is largely irrelevant.

I finally came to a point where I was willing to make ANY changes necessary to keep my serenity. Obviously, not drinking was one of them but there were many more. I stopped watching the news. I stopped listening to talk radio. I stopped arguing with people on Facebook and Twitter. I stopped trying to force my beliefs onto others.

In the real world, I ceased fighting... anything. I finally came to realize that none of the bickering (even if I was certain I was right) was worth losing my serenity. I paused. I stopped.

I came to understand that *99% of everything outside of my hula hoop is really none of my business and out of my control*.

Once I came to that understanding, life became much simpler.

Once the weight of the world was lifted from my shoulders, I was able to notice and appreciate the little things in life. The single yellow dandelion flower centered in a canvas of rich green grass. The sound of a waterfall. The peace I feel as much as see as a breeze whispers through the pines. The elderly lady who held a door open for me. The wag of a dog's tail.

After a while, and it took far less time than I would

have expected, I couldn't help see God's presence everywhere. No, I haven't been 'born again' and I still don't attend church, but the God of my understanding has been there all along; beside me, around me, and within me. I was simply too filled with negativity and anger to notice.

Today, despite life's challenges, I am able to live a life of gratitude.

Chapter Nine

PROGRESS, NOT PERFECTION

Recovery is a journey. Despite the rosy picture, my journey isn't over yet. I have moments where my old habits and character defects reappear. There are times I still get angry. The difference today is that I don't hold on to it. I have learned to let go. Conflicts and emotions that the 'old me' would have stewed on for days, now last just minutes instead.

The tools that I have learned and acquired through the steps of AA allow me to deal with life on life's terms.

One of the greatest gifts has been an enhanced level of self-awareness. Let's be honest, there is a plethora of stupidity in the world, and I can't do anything about any of it. But I can, if I am honestly self-aware, do something about how I react to it. I no longer allow a few seconds of some stupid interaction (occasionally propagated by me) ruin the rest of my day.

I let it go... most of the time.

I am not perfect, just ask my wife. Sometimes my ego puffs back up. Especially at home. There are even times where I intentionally try to stir things up, just because chaos was such a natural part of my old life. But soon, the self-awareness kicks in. I pull myself back from the abyss, make amends, and then get on with my day.

One of the tools that I have used since the beginning is a prayer called the Serenity Prayer. You will hear it at most meetings. It is the simplest way to get me calm and refocused on doing the right things and reacquiring my serenity.

God, grant me the serenity to accept the things I cannot change,
the courage to change the things I can, and
the wisdom to know the difference.

This little prayer can be uttered in seconds, almost anywhere, and it works every time. The first line reminds me that I am not in control, there are things that I don't like. I am going to repeat something I wrote about earlier, because it was hugely important to my sobriety.

99% of everything outside of my hula hoop is none of my business.

The second line reminds me that I do have the power to change a few things...my thoughts, my actions, and my reactions.

The last line tells me that I cannot control someone else's actions or behaviors (or nearly anything else in life), and I have to be smart enough to remember that. My ego needs to be kept in check from time to time. The wisdom in that prayer refers to learning to live god's will for me, not my own will. My will caused a great many problems in my life.

You will often hear people in the rooms use the saying: *Let go, and let God.* That's the shorthand version of the same thing.

Acceptance is the key. I have to accept life as it is, for that is the only way I can cease fighting everything. Everything else I turn over to my higher power with the full faith and confidence that everything will work out EXACTLY the way it is supposed to... whether I like it or not.

The Big Book tells us that "we claim spiritual progress, rather than spiritual perfection", which is true for a number of reasons. First of all, we are all human. We all have times where we are not as centered and selfless as we would like to be. We all have occasions and life events that pull us away from the program, even only (hopefully) temporarily. We all have times where we must question our motives, or make amends.

My daily goal as I attempt to practice these principles in all of my affairs is simple:

I don't need to be better than anyone else,
I just try to be a better guy today, than I was yesterday.

If I can live up to that, if I can string some of those days together, I know I am on the right path.

I hope I never reach a point where I feel like I have perfected this program. I hope I always keep myself open to new spiritual growth opportunities. I pray that I never forget where I came from and consider myself 'cured'. For if I do, my ego has won. My openness and willingness to continue to learn and grow are what keep me grounded.

There will even be those within the program that will say that just by having written this book, my ego has taken over.

As with most things, I cannot control how people take this book or react to it. I only can examine my own motives and goals. My intent was not to puff myself up, but to give those of you teetering on the edge a look into the rooms of AA, and explain some of the things that kept me out of the rooms for far too long. My goal was to tell those of you considering coming to AA what it is, and what it isn't. It was to share some of my experiences, my strength, and perhaps most importantly... HOPE.

There is an easier softer way. There is a way to recovery. There is a way to end the chaos and find peace.

But you must take action, the first of which is to put the bottle down and find a meeting of Alcoholics Anonymous.

I pray you find peace and serenity in your life.

www.ingramcontent.com/pod-product-compliance
Lightning Source LLC
Chambersburg PA
CBHW071848020426
42331CB00007B/1905